I0845500

The Legal Magic Mushrooms of North America: A Study of the Amanita muscaria Varieties

Written by Carl E. Miller and Lily Jo White

Published by Volunteers Variety

The purpose of this book is to document numerous aspects of the legal magic mushrooms that grow wild in North America. In no way do I recommend that any person consume these mushrooms, however to learn more about them, somebody has to experiment with them— so I will be that somebody. These mushrooms are technically considered poisonous as well as hallucinogenic, although just how poisonous is greatly debated.

I will not only be studying the effects of these legal magic mushrooms, but also their growing habitat, distribution range, life cycle, potential cultivation and much more. Now most people who think about the term "magic mushrooms" automatically assume that they must be illegal, which is usually true— however this depends on the type of magic mushrooms. Psilocybe mushrooms, which contain the active drugs psilocybin and psilocin, are illegal; to both cultivate and possess.

But this does not apply to arguably the most easily identifiable magic mushrooms in the world, Amanita muscaria. If you are a fan of my writing then you may find yourself wondering why I am even using the term magic mushrooms, after I've stated numerous times that I wasn't too fond of the term—however after much consideration I ultimately changed my stance. Some mushrooms truly are magic, and to attempt to put another label on them would be disingenuous.

So what exactly makes an Amanita muscaria mushroom different from most traditional magic mushrooms in terms of legality? Well, if you find yourself asking this question, then rest assured you are about to have your answer. The main difference is, the active drugs in Amanita muscaria are not psilocybin or psilocin, but instead muscimol and ibotenic acid, with trace amounts of muscarine. These drugs are not regulated in most of the United States.

Although these legal drugs produce hallucinogenic effects, it's also fair to point out that it comes with a little bit more of a risk. Not much is known about muscimol and ibotenic acid, or muscarine for that matter— but research into the drugs has increased as of late. One thing that most researchers have unanimously concluded is that in high doses, ibotenic acid can be a neurotoxin; which means the drug can be destructive to nerves.

Ibotenic acid is also used as a "brain-lesioning drug", which initially made me very nervous about the mushroom altogether until I researched the matter further. Upon further investigation is when I realized that this was only the case when the drug was injected into the brain of mice. I have no plans of injecting anything (I hate needles), especially not directly into my brain, so my concern naturally decreased.

When the Amanita muscaria mushroom is dried, supposedly a decent amount of the ibotenic acid (roughly 30%) is converted to muscimol, which is undeniably the safer of the two drugs—although the validity of the conversion is debated. I've also read countless stories of people consuming the mushrooms fresh, in rather large amounts, but this comes with some serious risks. These risks cannot simply be dismissed, they must be taken very seriously.

Some people only reported minor negative side effects with large doses; such as nausea and a headache. But there have also been reports of strokes, seizures and sometimes even people entering a coma-like state for a brief period after consuming large amounts of

Amanita muscaria. Although extreme side effects are very rare, most experts will say this mushroom is not recommended for human consumption! This also goes for other mushrooms that contain muscimol and ibotenic acid, such as the more potent Amanita pantherina species (which is usually a dark brown with white warts).

I will test these mushrooms using extreme caution, but extreme caution should be used for nearly anything you consume, and only a fool would try to convince you otherwise. In life, you only get one body and one mind, so we better be careful with how we conduct ourselves. I became fascinated with Amanita muscaria about a decade ago, while living in Cleveland, Ohio. At the time, I had no clue how I would ever get a hold of these mushrooms and try them for myself— so I stuck to psilocybin.

I became rather good at growing different types of mushrooms indoors, but I'm fully aware that not one single person has had luck growing these Amanita muscaria mushrooms indoors. This is mainly because they are a mycorrhizal fungi, meaning they form a symbiotic (give and take) relationship with specific plants and trees. This is a rather difficult scenario to attempt to recreate indoors, but I believe I will do it someday.

So that leaves us with the main question, where can you find Amanita muscaria? Well these mushrooms can be found all throughout the world, but I will keep this article confined to North America. I have gotten extremely lucky with the area that I moved to, in the Appalachian foothills in Ohio— right in the tri-state area of OH-WV-PA. The reason I love this area is simple; it's beautiful here, I can travel 15 minutes south or east and be in a different state, and mushrooms truly thrive in this environment.

So below is a North America distribution range map for Amanita muscaria that I made, basing it somewhat off of a few others that I've seen, along with information that I've gathered on where they are typically found. I've read a lot of conflicting information in regards to the safety of these mushrooms, and the same can be said about where they grow. But nevertheless, I have found them numerous times so far this year.

AMANITA MUSCARIA
N. AMERICA
DISTRIBUTION
RANGE MAP

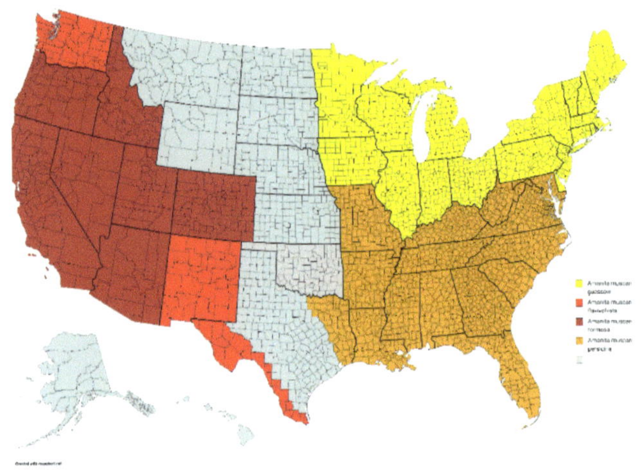

AMANITA MUSCARIA VAR. GUESSOWI
AMANITA MUSCARIA SUBSP. FLAVIVOLVATA
AMANITA MUSCARIA VAR. FORMOSA
AMANITA MUSCARIA VAR. PERSICINA

First off, you will have to either spend a lot of time in the woods, or get lucky. Second, you will want to search for specific trees that they are associated with. In my area, they seem to enjoy growing near Eastern White Pines, Oaks, and Spruce; with Spruce seemingly the ideal choice. I've spent close to 200 hours in the woods this year, photographing and documenting different mushroom species in the tri-state area. I've identified more than 100 species for a separate book, and Amanita muscaria was one of the harder finds.

When I finally found the mushroom, towards the end of September (70° highs and 45° lows) , I was beyond excited. This was a huge relief for me, as I wouldn't consider finishing my book on wild mushrooms if I didn't find that species, that's how important it was to me. The first one I found was very young, and very bright yellow (with a hint of orange). This was not your classic Amanita muscaria with the red cap and white warts, this was instead a variety with the scientific name Amanita muscaria var. guessowii. This species typically grows in late Summer and Autumn in North America.

Shortly after discovering the mushroom I found another under the same giant Spruce tree, so I decided to observe the life cycle over the course of several days since it wasn't far from my home. But I was unaware just how much slugs enjoy these mushrooms specifically. I've been in a constant battle with these bastard slugs since I began studying wild mushrooms, but the way they eat the Amanita muscaria was quite different. They literally devour these mushrooms, then seemingly pass out in some sort of trance-like Amanita dream.

Despite my slug problem, I was still able to observe most of the life cycle and get most of the mushroom home intact, with only a few slug holes to work around. But some of the other smaller mushrooms I was hoping to allow to grow larger, were completely eaten upon returning. I was happy and sad at the same time with my first Amanita muscaria find. I was happy to find the mushroom that I've long dreamed of finding, but a bit sad I didn't find more.

Now a lot of people think the classic red and white Amanita muscaria is the coolest looking mushroom in the world, but I truly believe the coolest one is the Amanita muscaria var. guessowii. This mushroom, with it's bright yellowish-orange glow and white warts, is incredible to look at. The mushroom was glowing with mystique under that Spruce tree, and even holding it felt magical. So let's take a look at a bit of the growing environment and life cycle.

The specific variety of the Amanita muscaria species (Amanita muscaria var. guessowii) was first described by the variant name guessowii in 1933, was named after Canadian botanist and author, Hans Theodor Güssow. But admiring these mushrooms in the wild is so rare, that we must discover a way to cultivate these mushrooms indoors— so later in the book we will take a look at what that would consist of.

After my discovery, I began to hunt for more the following week, and to my great surprise I found a very large Amanita persicina— which was originally thought to be of the Amanita muscaria genus, but recent DNA results show it is better fit as it's own distinct species. This mushroom, as you can see in the distribution map, is usually found in the Southeastern United States, as far North as West Virginia. But being in the tri-state area, I was fortunate to find it in an open field, although the cap was about half-way eaten, likely by a deer.

Deer eating Amanita muscaria mushrooms dates back a long way to Serbian reindeer, which some people cite as the origins of the story of Santa Claus traveling with flying reindeer. The Amanita-inspired Christmas theory would go even further when comparisons were made to Christmas ornaments, and Amanita muscaria mushrooms hanging from pine trees to dry— which would later be distributed as gifts.

These are the same mushrooms that are featured in the Mario franchise, where Mario grows larger after eating the mushroom. Amanita muscaria mushrooms are also what inspired Alice in Wonderland, and many other strange fairy tales and folklore throughout history.

The Amanita persicina species was first
described in 1977 by Dav. T. Jenkins,

but at that time it was considered a variety of Amanita muscaria. The mushroom is known to only grow with Oak or Pine, so again cultivation of this species will also prove to be incredibly difficult. But the same was said for Morchella mushrooms, aka Morels, however now indoor cultivation of these mushrooms have led to a multimillion dollar industry. If you think about it, the same exact stuff was being said about growing Morels. The issue was they are mycorrhizal, similar to Amanita muscaria.

To bypass this issue, some growers have used mulched wood as a bulk substrate, while more recently new techniques are emerging. In 2021, news broke that growers have had success for the first time cultivating black Morels, which are usually even harder to find in the wild than the others. They reported using grass as the symbiotic plant, and having tremendous success. This leads to a discovery that I made while working on a book about the phenomenon of mushrooms growing in graveyards. I found that most of these mushrooms growing in the cemeteries that I visited were connected to a plant called Vinca minor; especially the Chanterelle mushrooms.

So Vinca minor serves as a definite host plant for Chanterelles and likely Morels, but I believe they may also be the key to growing Amanita muscaria varieties, and especially Amanita persicina. This is mainly because I found Amanita persicina growing in an open field, not necessarily close to any specific tree, seeming to more closely associate with grass. So let's look at the Vinca minor plant before continuing to discuss the possibilities of cultivation.

Now a greenhouse grow might be the right choice to attempt this, and I truly believe the deep-rooting Vinca minor plant is going to be a major contributing factor for indoor mushroom cultivation for the mycorrhizal types in the future. Instead of using a sample of the active mycelium from where you find the mushroom, you can always use the preferred method— cloning. This may sound difficult, but no need to worry.

The best way to easily clone the mushroom is the cardboard method, along with using agar dishes. So first you will take some cardboard and cut it into small square pieces.Then you will pull the mushroom and have a sterile knife ready. You will want to cut several small pieces of the flesh of the cap near the stem, along with small parts of the stem; preferably all in one slice each time. You can then take the cardboard squares and soak them in cold water. After this step is complete, you will place the pieces of mushroom flesh in between the cardboard squares, stacking the squares during the process.

Not too much is needed, just five or six pieces should do the trick. The goal is to simply get some active mycelium growing, after that is accomplished we can always increase the amount of mycelium by introducing more cardboard, or some sort of other substrate. The cardboard should be placed in a fruiting chamber with the correct, dark and cool environment being established. Within a few days, you should see some strong mycelium growth which can then be transferred to a better bulk substrate.

So when looking at mycorrhizal fungi, we have to try to better understand what exactly is occuring. The fungal network is serving as a means for plants and fungi to exchange proteins and nutrients. So with Amanita muscaria, the goal is simple, yet complicated. In order to cultivate this species, you will have to find an alternate way to get these important nutrients to the fungi. I will continue to research this matter further, but I know it's a long road to perfection. One thing that gives me the most hope is that in some countries Amanita muscaria is considered an invasive species— so if we can discover the cause of this, then it can be very beneficial.

So now what? I've found the mushrooms that I've long been searching for, and I've researched them enough to feel confident in consuming them, kind of… Again the conflicting information in regards to the preparation does cause some concern. I've read a lot about parboiling them, or heating them in a low temperature in the oven. All of this seems to be an attempt at decarboxylating the mushroom.

Some people also enjoy mixing the mushrooms into a brew, such as tea or wine. The theory with the wine is if you use pasteurized grape juice, you can take a small pinch of the dried mushroom cap and add it to the grape juice, which will then turn into a liquid culture, or active mycelium. This makes some think of the biblical sacred wine. Other theories suggest that placing the mushroom in milk can be used to lower the toxicity, while some people use alcohol to increase the effects.

I personally felt more confident in drying them in front of a fan (like I typically do with other mushrooms) and briefly in front of a space heater, until they were cracker dry— then I stored them in a mason jar with moisture-absorbent packets. I decided that first I would smoke some of the mushrooms in a pipe, then on a separate day I would eat some and make comparisons with the effects.

The caps are supposedly the part of the mushroom that contains most of the drugs present, so that was what I focused on, although I kept one stem as well, the other was too damaged by slugs. Some reports suggest a decent amount of the drugs are also present in the bulb of the stem, so I will try that and report back. But for now, I will report on smoking the caps. I mixed a little bit of caps from both types of mushrooms, Amanita muscaria var. guessowii and Amanita persicina.

At first I took a small hit from the pipe, admittedly somewhat nervous about what the results might be. But after a little hesitation, I took a much larger second hit and that was when the magic occurred. I was watching a baseball game on TV, and immediately I became ultra-focused. The screen began to seemingly pulsate and I felt like the television was zooming in and and out; getting closer in distance, then further, then closer again. I hit the pipe for a third time and stumbled outside, and once outside everything seemed extremely bright.

This brightness was almost too much, it was the middle of the afternoon and I decided to head back inside. I watched TV for a while longer, then as night approached I took a fourth hit from the pipe. After this fourth hit I was feeling incredible, a huge rush which was quickly followed by ultimate relaxation. I decided to lay in bed and watch an old Italian Giallo film that was dubbed in English. During the movie I fell asleep, and then I entered that trance-like Amanita dream state that I encountered the slugs experiencing— and I must say, it's hard to blame them.

When I awoke it was still dark outside, so I took another hit from the pipe and headed back out to look at the moon. Incredible, a truly amazing sight while under the influence of Muscimol. Many stars were out that night as well, and the entire scene was very pleasant. I would say I felt the effects of the drug in waves with some strange, mild visuals, and the duration was roughly an hour or two after the last hit— though seemingly longer. Many reports suggest the effects are felt for far longer when eaten compared to smoked. However as I mentioned earlier, that does come with more risk.

According to many scientific studies, muscimol is a GABAA receptor agonist, compared to psilocybin stimulating serotonin receptors. Although recent studies also suggest that at least when tested on rats, muscimol causes a rise in serotonin levels too. This study seems to back up the conclusion that many others have reached from personal usage, myself included. Muscimol, and perhaps ibotenic acid to a lesser degree, definitely seem to alter your serotonin levels, based on my experience.

Although the drug produced a great hallucinogenic effect, while also seemingly raising serotonin levels— the comparisons with psilocybin seem to be few. Most ethnomycologists (mushroom historians) have tracked the earliest origins of Amanita muscaria to Siberia, however author R. Gordon Wasson has presented evidence that shows this theory is a little bit more complicated. For instance, Wasson details the earlier usage of these mushrooms in North America in an article titled Traditional Use in North America of Amanita muscaria for Divinatory Purposes.

In said article, Wasson writes about a letter sent from a Superior of the Jesuit Order from Quebec, Canada named Père Charles l'Allemant. The letter was sent to his brother in France, and within the letter was this translated verbatim quote: "They assure you that after death they go to heaven where they eat mushrooms and hold intercourse with each other". The author says with certainty that the mushrooms mentioned were in fact Amanita muscaria, and the letter was dated 1626, a century earlier than the first documented reports in Siberia.

So about a week after smoking some of the mushrooms, I decided it was time to eat some. I ate a few pieces of the cap and stem (roughly 1g), chewing on them for quite some time. Most of it tasted very plain, I actually tasted them far more when smoking them. When smoked, they had a real earthy taste and smell. The high came on fairly quickly after I ate them, and at the 45 minute mark I began feeling much larger in size, briefly. This was followed by a very odd, somewhat numb, tingling feeling on my gums.

Again, everything became very bright, similar to when I smoked it.
I found many of the effects to be very similar to smoking the mushrooms, with perhaps more of an initial rush after eating them. This was actually another similarity that I have found with psilocybin, the feeling of a sudden rush through your body. Some light visuals accompanied this feeling too, especially when I closed my eyes. This euphoric feeling lasted for about 4 hours, then I decided to smoke a little to go with it. This definitely recharged my high, for lack of a better term.

The visuals were definitely different from other hallucinogenic drugs, somewhat mild at low doses, but with unique geometrical shapes and patterns, especially with my eyes closed— however I must also note that a slight headache does seem to occur after both smoking, and eating the mushrooms. The headache is very slight, occuring only in very brief intervals; almost unnoticeable but still worth documenting for the purpose of accuracy.

After enjoying my night thoroughly, I decided to go to sleep; secretly wishing for more Amanita dreams. My wishes came true, only this time I felt like I was awake while dreaming. It was a mental state that I've never quite experienced before, but I found the experience extremely pleasant. A movie was playing in the background, and I was nodding off and waking up throughout it.

The feeling was almost like I've stayed up for too many days, and now sleeping was inevitable. Every time I dozed off I entered a new dream, one that was completely different than the previous dream. I found both smoking and eating the mushrooms to be extremely enjoyable, but all in all, I think my preferred method would be to smoke the mushrooms.

While smoking, I think it's easier to gauge how much you need, and receive a relatively similar high with a lot less risk, in my opinion. However these mushrooms have been studied so little that it's impossible for me to say that with certainty. I found the drugs muscimol and ibotenic acid to be very unique, and they produce some very strange closed-eyed visuals. I don't think my trip would be considered quite as colorful as psilocybin or LSD, but the geometrical shapes and patterns were definitely present.

I've taken far larger doses of just about every hallucinogenic drug you can imagine, however safety was of concern with consuming these— so I didn't go full throttle with the dosage. I played it safe, essentially, and I think that was the correct choice. I was still able to gauge the effects of the mushrooms, while also minimizing any possible adverse reactions, such as seizures or going into a coma. This may sound extreme, but these are in fact listed as possibilities with large doses— although still remaining very rare.

Many researchers believe the coloring of the mushroom is due to the drugs they contain, but again I've read conflicting information on just which drug is causing this coloration; muscimol or ibotenic acid. I find this rather interesting, because once again we can make the rare comparison to psilocybe mushrooms. With psilocybe mushrooms, the drugs psilocybin and psilocin are responsible for the blue bruising that occurs— with the deep bruising indicating that more of the drugs are present.

I truly believe Amanita muscaria, and more specifically the drug muscimol, are going to play a major factor in the world of hallucinogens in the very near future. This prediction of mine is hardly

Nostradamus-level, as even recently a Canadian startup company (Psyched Wellness) began to work on creating extracts of Amanita muscaria to sell. There are numerous websites that already sell Amanita muscaria products, legally, however this company seems to be taking more of a scientific approach— even involving the National Research Council of Canada.

I'm sure that as more studies are conducted, scientists will discover even more drugs that are active in Amanita muscaria. For example, gaboxadol is a drug that is derived from muscimol that has been extensively studied for the "deep sleep" properties they are believed to possess. The future is bright for this mushroom, almost as bright as the cap. But there will be some obstacles to overcome, and some issues to iron out.

The main issue I see that has emerged, is that most of the Amanita muscaria advocates are seemingly just approaching this species with giggles and goofiness. This type of behavior will only slow down the amount of research that is being conducted, and possibly lead to the drug being outlawed. Although the saying is "all publicity is good publicity", I don't find that to always be factual, especially when airheads are promoting a very unique and legal drug.

The tuning-out crowd who can't handle their drugs, will ultimately be the end of legal drugs. This same rinse and repeat crowd are somewhat to blame for most hallucinogenic drugs being made illegal in the first place. Now I like to get good and high as much as the next guy, and even space out from time to time— but I'd rather treat these drugs like the mind-expansion tools that they really are.

After my research was conducted, I would have to say that although the effects are not quite as fascinating as psilocybin, they are still very interesting and unique. I plan on working with these mushrooms a lot moving forward, and hopefully becoming the first person to cultivate them indoors. I truly believe the potential is limitless with this species, and the Amanita muscaria var. guessowii is the greatest looking mushroom in the world, in my opinion.

The End

Afterword

Both species, the Amanita muscaria var. guessowii and Amanita persicina were found in Eastern Ohio, in the tri-state area (OH-WV-PA). These mushrooms are also going to be featured in a future book of mine titled Wild Mushrooms of Ohio and Northern Appalachia: A Field Guide for Beginners. In the book, I photograph and describe more than 100 species of mushrooms— and I'm aiming for an early 2023 release date.

More From The Author
(Mushrooms of the Grave)
(How to Grow Psilocybin Mushrooms:
The Complete Beginners Guide to
Indoor Cultivation)
(Psychedelic Drugs and the Ultimate
Pursuit for Mind Control)
(Bizarre: A Bad Trip Into Strangeness)
*(Wild Mushrooms of Ohio and Northern
Appalachia: A Field Guide for
Beginners)

www.ingramcontent.com/pod-product-compliance
Lightning Source LLC
Chambersburg PA
CBHW040903260726

48664CB00025B/1388